COLINET DE LANNOYS

MASS AND SONGS

Collection « Épitome musical »

responsable éditorial
Philippe VENDRIX

comité éditorial
Frank DOBBINS, Nicoletta GUIDOBALDI, François REYNAUD
Jean-Michel VACCARO, Philippe VENDRIX

© Éditions Klincksieck, 1999
ISBN 2-252-03215-4

CENTRE D'ÉTUDES SUPÉRIEURES DE LA RENAISSANCE
Collection « Épitome musical »

COLINET DE LANNOYS

MASS AND SONGS

Introduction and editions

Fabrice FITCH

KLINCKSIECK

1999

Gravure musicale
Vincent BESSON

Composition et mise en page
Patrick GILBERT

Révision et corrections
Frank DOBBINS, Philippe VENDRIX

TABLE OF CONTENTS

INTRODUCTION

COLINET DE LANNOYS is one of many fifteenth-century composers who enjoyed some renown in their own time, but of whom practically nothing is known today. His surviving output is limited to two short songs and three related Mass movements. The ascription to "Lanoys" in a manuscript copied in Prague[1] of a Credo and Sanctus was at first greeted cautiously on account of that source's relatively late date and haphazard compilation. But in 1989, a concordance was identified through a fragmentary cycle, preserved in the Roman manuscript San Pietro B80, which had recently been studied by Rob C. Wegman. In view of that source's closer proximity to those preserving Colinet's songs, a reappraisal of the Mass suggested itself; and though it remains incomplete, its stylistic profile has sufficient points of contact with the songs to warrant the publication of all three works side by side.

1. Life

The facts of Colinet's life have occasioned some confusion.[2] Though all the manuscript sources that give his Christian name refer to him as "Colin" or "Col[l]inet", he has tradi-

---

1   Hradec Králové Krajske Muzeum, Knihovna. MS II A 7 (Speciálník Codex), hereafter 'Spec'.

2   No summary of the hitherto accepted biography exists. The salient points are documented in Frank A. D'ACCONE, 'The Singers of San Giovanni in Florence during the 15th Century', *JAMS*, xiv (1962),

tionally been identified with one Charles or Karolus de Launoy (c.1456-1506), a singer active in Bourges and in Italy. But the names Charles and Colin are etymologically distinct (the latter being a diminutive of Nicolas). Further, Charles is known to have died in Florence in 1506,[3] whereas Guillaume Crétin's *Déploration* places "lannoys" in the company of composers having predeceased Johannes Ockeghem (d. 6 February, 1497).[4] There can be no doubt that Charles and our composer were two different individuals.[5] Whether Colinet was related to the two singers Jehan and David de Lannoys who served at the French royal chapel from the 1440s to the 1470s,[6] cannot be ascertained. The only document attesting to his activity dates from 6 February, 1497, when "colinet de lanoys" is granted safe-conduct to leave Milan along with several other singers in the aftermath of the assassination of Duke Galeazzo Maria Sforza late in the preceding year.[7] Nothing else is known of Colinet's existence.

2. The Mass

From the dating of its earlier source, San Pietro B80,[8] and judging by its stylistic attributes, one may place the composition of Colinet's Mass in the 1470s. The three voices have distinct ranges, with the upper voices often engaged in imitation at the unison (although the Discantus may find itself as much as an octave below the Tenor). The lower

---

    p. 344 fn. 180, and p. 350 fn. 203; F. A. D'ACCONE, 'Heinrich Isaac in Florence: New and Unpublished Documents', *MQ*, il (1963), pp. 471-2 and 479-480; F. A. D'ACCONE, 'The Musical Chapel at the Florentine Cathedral and Baptistery during the First Half of the 16th Century', *JAMS*, xxiv (1971), p. 9; Paula M. HIGGINS, 'Tracing the Careers of Late Medieval Composers: the Case of Philippe Basiron of Bourges', *AM*, lxii (1990), p. 15; and Edward E. LOWINSKY, 'Ascanio Sforza's Life: A Key to Josquin's Biography and an Aid to the Chronology of his Works', *Josquin Desprez. Proceedings of the International Josquin Festival-Conference, New York City, 21-25 June 1971*, ed. E. E. LOWINSKY in collaboration with Bonnie J. BLACKBURN (London, 1976), pp. 40-41. The most recent restatement of the Colinet/Carolus conflation is in Christopher A. REYNOLDS, *Papal Patronage and the Music of Saint Peter's, 1380-1513* (Berkeley, Los Angeles and London, 1995), pp. 228-9 and 237-8.

3   F. A. D'ACCONE, 'Heinrich Isaac in Florence...', *op. cit.*, pp. 471-2 and 479-80.

4   *Déploration de Guillaume Crétin sur le trépas de Jean Ockeghem*, ed. Ernest THOINAN, Paris: A. Claudin, 1864 (*R* London: H. Baron, 1965), pp. 5-6.

5   Incidentally, the documents relating to Carolus appear to give his surname as "Launoys", rather than "Lannoys"; but this detail may be inconclusive, for the letters "u" and "n" are easily confused in the script of the time. In any case, it is the discrepancy of Christian name that conclusively differentiates the two musicians.

6   Leeman L. PERKINS, 'Musical Patronage at the Royal Court of France under Charles VII and Louis XI (1422-1483)', *JAMS*, xxxvii (1984), pp. 546-57.

7   E. E. LOWINSKY, 'Ascanio Sforza's Life...', *op. cit.*, pp. 40-1.

8   The concordance in Spec was identified in Robert J. MITCHELL, 'The palaeography and repertory of Trent Codices 89 and 91, together with analyses and editions of six mass cycles by franco-flemish composers from Trent Codex 89', Ph.D. dissertation, University of Exeter, 1989, pp. 235-6.

voice has a supporting role, but its occasional involvement in imitation and its range mark it as a true Bassus. The movements' internal divisions are articulated by means of changes of mensuration from C to ¢. This arrangement is also found in works by Ockeghem and Martini, as well as in several anonymous works contained in the Codex Speciálník; but its combination with the three distinct ranges noted above lends the work a more distinctive morphological profile.[9] Fragmentary though it be, the Mass gives quite a clear idea of Colinet's style. Imitation predominates throughout, and the texture is generally transparent and uncomplicated. Harmonic rhythm is fairly staid, and points of imitation are based on resolutely triadic figures, so that even relatively lively melodic figures are circumscribed by their harmonic context. The overall impression is one of directness and simplicity.

The Mass tends to alternate two harmonic poles, G and B♭; the lines of demarcation between them are usually very clear, with E♭ serving as the most common pivot between the two. An especially characteristic feature is the Tenor's reinterpretation of its precadential note as a suspension, forcing an imperfect cadence at the fifth below.[10] This unusual trait occurs several times in the course of the work (*e.g.,* Credo, bars 17-18). As it stands, the cycle is further unified by the reappearance of certain motifs and points of imitation (*e.g.,* the one at bar 28 of the Credo, which recurs several times in the course if the Mass at several pitch-levels). If Colinet appears ill at ease in setting the long Credo text, he is better able to sustain melodic interest in the later, melismatic sections. His elaboration of a simple rhythmic figure in the Benedictus (setting the words "*qui venit*") is one of the work's most memorable passages. Indeed, the Mass has its share of the melodic charm that characterizes the composer's songs.

---

9   Ockeghem's Mass *Quinti toni* has ranges similar to those of Colinet's Mass, and the same exclusive use of binary mensurations. This combination of resemblances led Rob C. Wegman to propose a tentative attribution of the Mass to Ockeghem (Rob C. WEGMAN, 'An Anonymous Twin to Johannes Ockeghem's *Missa Quinti Toni* in San Pietro B 80', *TVNM*, xxxvii (1987), pp. 23-48). Wegman's study appeared before Robert Mitchell's identification of the Speciálník concordance established Colinet's authorship. This discovery naturally altered the situation, but it seems fair to say that a close comparison of *Quinti toni* and Colinet's Mass yields few points of contact beyond their morphological similarity. In particular, the composers' use of imitation differs: in Colinet's music it is the primary means of musical articulation, whereas Ockeghem subsumes it within the dense polyphonic framework that is typical of his style. Further, the breadth of phrase so characteristic of Ockeghem is conspicuously absent in Colinet's work. Finally, Colinet's writing is characterized by a relatively slow rate of harmonic change, whereas the flexibility of the Contra (Bassus) of *Quinti toni* results in a constantly shifting harmonic field. It may be suggested that Colinet's use of a binary mensuration-scheme may have been the result of acquaintance, not with Ockeghem, but with Martini, whose presence in Milan a few months before Colinet's supposed arrival there in 1476 is firmly documented. Martini's reworking of, and Mass setting on *Cela sans plus* indicates his interest in Colinet's work; it is not unreasonable to propose that the influence was mutual. On the Mass and its relationship to Ockeghem's, see also Andrew KIRKMAN, *The Three-Voice Mass in the Later Fifteenth and Early Sixteenth Centuries: Style, Distribution and Case-Studies* (New York and London, 1995), pp. 269-78. For more on the Martini/Colinet connection, see C. A. REYNOLDS, *Papal Patronage...,* op. cit., pp. 28-38; note, however, that Reynolds's adoption of the Colinet/Carolus conflation leads him to propose a slightly different (and, in my view, erroneous) biographical context for the composers' meeting.

10   This feature was first noted by Rob C. WEGMAN in an unpublished article, 'Okeghem and Launoy'. I thank Dr. Wegman for making his study available to me.

3. The songs

The recent notoriety of *Cela sans plus* seems to be based on Otto Gombosi's damning dismissal of it as *"entschieden die dünnflüssigste Komposition, die mir jemals begegnet ist [...] eine ärmliche, blutarme Komposition von minimaler Erfindung [...]"*.[11] That remark appears to judge Colinet's little song by aesthetic criteria wholly foreign to his style. As in the Mass, the emphasis is on directness and clarity. Besides, the song's basic premise - the unfolding, phrase by phrase, of a popular melody by two voices at the octave in alternation, accompanied by one or several free voices - is one of which Colinet's contemporaries made frequent use (see for example Isaac's *Mon pere m'a donné mari*, preserved alongside *Cela sans plus* in Florence, Banco Rari 229,[12] or Colinet's other surviving song, *Adieu naturlic leven mijn*). They must have thought highly of the piece, for they paid it the sincerest form of flattery: reworkings by Johannes Martini, Johannes Jappart, Rigamundus, and (still more significantly) Mass-settings based upon it by Martini and Jacob Obrecht, bear witness to its success. What may have attracted Colinet's contemporaries is *Cela sans plus*'s almost epigrammatic concision, or the tightly knit Contra that festoons the more straightforward exposition of the principal voices. One discerns in the clear alternation of two polarities (G in lines 1 and 4, C in lines 2 and 3) a strategy similar to the one played out in the Mass.

To judge by its sole surviving copy in Florence, Basevi 2439, *Adieu naturlic leven mijn* did not achieve the popularity of *Cela sans plus*. Yet it has much in common with its companion. Both set a popular song, using the same technique (mentioned above), the alternating statements of each line of text by the two principal voices, this time with two accompanying ones. One detail in particular appears to support Basevi's ascription to Colinet: the appearance of the peculiar cadential progression with 4-3 suspension in the Contra altus, previously noted in connection with the Mass. It occurs no fewer than three times in this short piece (bars 6-7, 35-6, 51-2), but does not figure in the other extant settings of the melody.[13] This would appear to be a favourite device of Colinet's, and militates against the possibility of there having been several composers named "Lannoys" (or the possibility that the names "Colinet" and "Lanoys" may have designated different composers). *Adieu naturlic* is longer than *Cela sans plus*. Although this reflects the length of the songs' respective models, it may also explain why the longer-winded setting failed to have the impact of the other. Both songs may be regarded as roughly coeval with the Mass, though *Adieu naturlic* may be slightly later, dating perhaps from the 1480s.

---

11 Otto GOMBOSI, *Jacob Obrecht: Eine stilkritische Studie* (Leipzig, 1925), pp. 76-7.

12 Florence, Biblioteca Nazionale Centrale, MS Banco Rari 229, ff. 3v-4. Modern edition in *A Florentine Chansonnier from the Time of Lorenzo the Magnificent. Florence, Biblioteca Nazionale Centrale, MS Banco Rari 229*, ed. Howard Mayer BROWN (Chicago and London, 1983), Music Volume, pp. 7-8.

13 Of particular interest in this connection is the anonymous setting in St. Gallen 461 (see below under *Related works*).

CRITICAL APPARATUS

i. The Mass

Sources

a) Vatican City, Biblioteca Apostolica Vaticana, Ms San Pietro B 80, ff. 21v-25 (fragment of Sanctus, complete Agnus). Facsimile in *Vatican City, Biblioteca Apostolica Vaticana, San Pietro B 80...* (New York and London, 1986). (SP)

b) Hradec Králové Krajske Muzeum Knihovna MS II A7, ff. b7v-b11 (pp. 48-55) (Credo and Sanctus). (Spec)

Modern edition

Transcription of Sanctus fragment and Agnus after SPB80 in Rob C. WEGMAN, 'An Anonymous Twin...', *op. cit*, pp. 38-48.

Ascription

"Lanoys" (Spec only).

Although SP is closer both in time and place to the probable archetype, and despite the notoriously haphazard and messy layout of Spec, it is the latter that contains the more satisfactory reading of the Sanctus. Accordingly, this edition uses Spec for its reading of this movement. The main variants concern SP's more liberal use of ornamentation and of filled-in passing-notes, which seems likely to reflect scribal preference. For the rest, there are the usual ligature and minor color variants, longer values broken up or preserved, and a nearly equal number of outright scribal errors in both sources. Due to the prominence throughout of the pitch *e♭* (enshrined in the key-signature), this edition refrains in principle from naturalizing it at cadences (as in bar 8 of the Credo) or elsewhere, even when the result is a tritone with the pitch *a* beneath it.

The texting of the Credo has posed special problems, and has had to be reconstructed. The underlay in Spec is in a crammed, crabbed shorthand that rarely fits the music, finishing abruptly at the words *"qui locutus est per prophetas Amen"*. It seems likely that the scribe worked from a source which had (at best) incipits only, and that he attempted to fit in as much text as possible, stopping when he ran out of space. This edition respects the incipits, and eliminates certain portions of text that were customarily omitted at the time (from *"Deum de Deo"* to *"de Deo vero"*, and from *"cujus regni"*... to *"peccatorum"*), resulting at least in a plausible solution. Occasionally, longer notes have been broken up to accommodate the text, or (more rarely) repetitions of the same pitch have been tied. This is warranted by the variant readings in the Sanctus. These changes are indicated by means of smaller notes and broken ties, respectively. Text variants are indicated only when different from the edition; no one source has been preferred.

Variants are from SP unless otherwise stated.

Credo (Spec only: emendations) *Superius* 56/2 g' *Tenor* 31/1 f' *Contra* 30/1 A 82/2 G 95/2 a 123/3 c

Text *Superius* texted throughout; stops at "prophetas Amen" *Tenor* partial texting after Superius *Contra* textless

Sanctus *Superius* (SP missing up to bar 75) 12/2 orig 3 *br* 93/2 c' b'*sm* 99/3 a'*dot.mn,* g'*sm* 103-4 lig 135-9 no lig 141/3 b'*dot.mn* a'*sm* 146 lig 147-9 c"*L* d" *m.c.* *br* 151/1 g' 155 e'*dot.mn* d'*sm* 161 no lig 172/4 no *m.c.* *Tenor* 13/4 no *m.c* 15/3 e' d'*f* 41/2 2*mn* 44/1 a (Spec, emend. after SP) 60/1 2*sb* 62/1 *br* 63/1 no *m.c.* 65/1 *br* 67/5 f' (Spec, emend. after SP) 94/2 *m.c.* 100/2-3 g'*mn* 107/1-2 c'*mn* 108/4 c'*mn, sm* 116 2*sb* 119 *m.c.* 132-4 lig g*L* abr 143/2 no lig 151-2 lig 2*br* *Contra* 20/2-3 *sb* 22/1-3 f*mn* e*sm* 25/2 no *m.c.* 32/1 no lig 34/1 no lig 52 lig 59/3 Contra breaks off until 75 70/2 F (Spec. emend.) 79/1-2 e*dot.mn* d*sm* c*mn* (Spec., emend. after SP) 90/2 2*br* (Spec, emend. after SP) 93/2-4 Sp has G*dot.mn* F*sm* G*mn*; Spec has B*dot.mn* A*sm* G*mn, dot.mn* F*sm* G*mn* (emended by disregarding the last three notes of Spec) 118 g'*br* (Spec) 125/1 *m.c.* 128/1 *m.c.* 138-140 lig G*L* A*br* 141-3 lig 146/1 lig e' d'*sb* 153/4 no lig 155/3-156/3 missing (Spec) 161-4 6 *br* rests instead of 4 (Spec) 168/3 lig d e*sb*

Text *Superius* 23/2 Deus (Spec) 32/1 Sabaoth (Spec) 41/1 sunt (Spec) 41/2 celi (Spec) 51/4 terra (Spec) 72/2 tua (Spec) 99/2 excelsis (SP) 135/1 in (SP) 141/1 nomine (SP) 164/4 Domini (SP) *Tenor* 30/1 Sabaoth (Spec, SP) 40/3 sunt (Spec) 41/1 celi et terra (Spec) 41/1 celi (SP) 52/1 et terra (SP) [gloria tua, omitted in Spec] 73/2 tua (Spec) 75/1 Spec has incipit only for Osanna 98/1 in excelsis (SP) 102/1 Spec has incipit only for Benedictus 135/1 nomine (SP) 163/2 Domini (SP) *Contra* Spec is textless to 51/1; SP has incipit only 37/1 Pleni (SP) 51/1 et terra (SP), gloria tua (Spec) 75/1 Osanna (Spec has incipit only) 102/1 Benedictus qui venit (Spec) [qui venit in, omitted in SP] 145/1 nomine (SP) 165/1 Domini (SP)

Agnus (SP only) *Superius* 10/1 a (emend.) 54/2 g (emend.) *Tenor* 13/2 **#** before b 19/4 d' (emend.) *Contra* 81/82 punct. div. 88-9 punct. div.

Text *Superius* 50/2 tollis 62/1 peccata mundi 119/1 mundi 134/1 pacem *Tenor* 21/1 mundi [miserere nobis, omitted] 39/2 Dei 42/1 qui 42/4 tollis [peccata mundi miserere nobis, omitted] 117/2 mundi 126/1 dona 129/3 nobis *Contra* [peccata mundi miserere nobis, omitted] 51/2 tollis [peccata mundi miserere nobis, omitted] 116/2 mundi 124/1 dona

ii. Cela sans plus

Sources

a) Bologna, Civico museo bibliografico musicale MS Q 16, ff. 37v-38 (BQ16)

b) Bologna, Civico museo bibliografico musicale MS Q 17, ff. 19v-20 (BQ17)

c) Florence, Biblioteca Nazionale Centrale, Ms. Magl. XIX 176, ff. Ov-1 (Fl176)

d) Florence, Biblioteca Nazionale Centrale, Ms. Magl. XIX 178, ff. 39v-40 (Fl178)

e) Florence, Biblioteca Nazionale Centrale, MS Banco Rari 229, ff. 100v-101 (Fl229)

f) Rome, Biblioteca Casanatense, Cod. 2856, ff. 152v-153 (Cas)

g) Seville, Catedral Metropolitano, Biblioteca capitular y Colombina MS 5-1-43, ff. 54v-55 (Sev)

h) Vatican City, Biblioteca Apostolica Vaticana, Cappella Giulia, Cod. XIII, 27, ff. 79v-80 (CG)

i) Washington, Library of Congress, MS. M2. I M6 Case, ff. 12v-13 (Wol); facs. in Johannes WOLF, *Handbuch der Notationskunde* (Leipzig, 1913), i, p. 394

Prints

a) *Canti B. numero cinquanta* (Venice: O. Petrucci, 1502), ff. 19v-20 (Pet)

b) *Quinquagena carmina* (Mainz: P. Schofer, 1513), p. 16 [Tenor only] (Scho)

c) *[Lieder zu 3 & 4 Stimmen]* (Frankfurt am Main: C. Egenolff, ca 1535, no. 23 [Discantus only] (Ege)

Modern editions

Johannes WOLF, *Handbuch der Notationskunde* (Leipzig, 1913), i, p. 395-7

— *Werken van Jacob Obrecht, Wereldlijke Werke*, ed. J. WOLF (Amsterdam and Leipzig, 1908-21), pp. 83-84 (after Cas)

— Helen HEWITT, *Ottaviano Petrucci, Canti B numero cinquanta* (Chicago and London, 1967), pp. 137-9

— Howard M. BROWN, *A Florentine Chansonnier from the Time of Lorenzo the Magnificent. Florence, Biblioteca Nazionale Centrale, MS Banco Rari 229* (Chicago and London, 1983), Music Volume, pp. 198-200

— Thomas WARBURTON, 'Sicher's "Johannes Zela zons plus": A Problem of Identity', *AM*, lv (1983), pp. 84-88 (after Cas)

— *New Obrecht Edition*, ed. Chris MAAS *et al.*, (Utrecht, 1993), XIII, pp. 13-14 (after Pet)

Ascription

"Collinet de Lanoy" (Fl229); "Colinet delanoy" (BQ17); "Colinet de Lannoy" (Cas., with fourth voice ascribed to "Jo. Martini"); "Colinet" (CG); "Lannoy" (Pet, Scho); "par de Lannoy" (Wol, in two different hands); "Josquin" (Fl178)

Clefs

All sources have G2 C3 C3, except Fl178 (G3 C3 C2)

Key signature

♮♮♮ (BQ17, Fl176, Fl178, Fl229, Sev); ♭♮♮ (CG and Wol, with flat on *f''* in top voice of Wol); ♭♭♭ (BQ16); ♮♮♮♮ with flat on *f''* in top voice (Pet); ♭♭♭♭ (Cas)

Fl178's ascription to Josquin presumably confuses Colinet's song with Josquin's eponymous setting.[13] As far as the musical text is concerned most sources agree, disregarding the usual inessential details. The following exceptions are worth noting.

i. Pet and Cas have a fourth voice, ascribed in Cas to Martini. Many of the variants in Cas are attributable to its instrumental destination (see Lewis B. LOCKWOOD, *Music in Renaissance Ferrara 1440-1505* (Oxford, 1984), pp. 269 ff.). One significant variant at the end of the Contra appears to be a corruption. For these reasons, Cas has been disregarded in establishing the musical text, and the fourth voice has not been included.

ii. Only one part-book survives for Scho and Ege; the latter is a reprint of Pet, and Ege has several pieces drawn from it. For this reason, neither has been included in the critical apparatus.

iii. A scribal error in Wol (Tenor) elides phrases 2 and 3, though its reading is otherwise sound.

This edition follows Fl176, with only two emendations. If one disregards ligature and color variants, its reading exactly matches that of Pet (barring one corruption in the latter), while the manuscript sources offer no cumulative evidence against it.

The issue of musica ficta in *Cela sans plus* is particularly perplexing. Complete sources differ as to the placement of flats in both the key-signature and the body of the text. Five give none whatsoever, but the other five have one flat in at least one voice, entailing extensive editorial ficta in the other voices. The reworkings by other composers do little to clarify matters, for neither Obrecht's Mass nor Martini's have flat-signatures; there is nothing in the music to prevent a mixolydian performance of *Cela sans plus*. However, the fact that even those sources that have no flats in the signature carry some in the music (while differing as to their placement), suggests that a signature-flat in all voices is possible. In order to provide a faithful picture of these divergences, and since no one reading can claim precedence, this edition adopts a flexible approach. There is no flat in the signature; instead, each occurence of a flat in the music *in any source* is indicated in bold type *above the staff* with a number in square brackets. The numbers refer to a list of flat variants separate from the other variants. Other instances of ficta are editorial, but most are a direct consequence of flats in the sources (*e.g.,* Wol's flat at bar 6 of the Tenor entails those at bars 10, 41 and 45, and at bars 4, 8, 39 and 43 of the Discantus; these account for most occurences of the pitch-class *b*. Note, however, that the flat in the Tenor at bar 6 in Wol, reported by both Brown and Hewitt, is not visible in the facsimile of Wol in J. WOLF, *Handbuch... op. cit.*). In this way, performers can experiment with both solutions, and the various

---

13 See the *New Josquin Edition*, xxvii, ed. Jaap VAN BENTHEM and H. M. BROWN (Utrecht: Vereniging voor de Nederlandse Muziekgeschiedenis, 1987–), Critical Commentary, pp. 27-9, for a brief discussion of the spurious ascription of Colinet's piece to Josquin.

points between, reflected in individual sources. (See also H. M. BROWN, *A Florentine Chansonnier,* *op. cit.,* Music Volume, p. 200, fn. 1.)

The text, also taken from Fl176, has been emended:

Cela sans plus et puis hola!	Only this much, and then bye-bye.
Gente bergiere belle de bon renom,	Sweet shepherdess, beauty of good repute,
Getes mon cuer hors de vos [vostre] prison.	cast my heart out from your prison.
Cela sans plus et puis hola!	Only this much, and then bye-bye!

Music   *Superius* 9 *br* (Wol)   11/1-3 f' *e'sm* f'*sb* (BQ17, Fl229, Wol)   14 *dot.br* (BQ17)   15 lig (BQ16)   16 *dot.br* (BQ17, CG)   19/4-20/1 b'*mn* e''*sb* (Sev)   20/2 *m.c.* (CG)   24 no *col* (BQ17, Fl229, Sev, CG, Wol, Pet)   26 *L* (Wol); *br* 2*sb* (CG)   30/2 no *m.c.* (BQ16, BQ17, Fl178, Pet)   31/2-3 c''*dot.mn* b' b' a'*sm* (Fl178)   39 lig d'' b'*sb* a'*br* (BQ16)   45 no lig (BQ17, Fl178, Fl229, Sev, Pet)   45/2 g'*dot.sb* e'*mn* f'*sb* (BQ17)   46/1-3 f' *e'sm* f'*sb* (Fl229, Sev, Wol)   *Tenor* 6 lig (BQ16)   11 lig a *gbr,* *gbr* (Wol)   16 *dot.br* (BQ17, CG)   17 lig c' d'*sb* (BQ16); lig c' d'*sb* e' *br* (Wol)   18 *dot.br* (BQ17, CG)   19 lig e' f'*sb* (BQ16); lig e' f'*sb* g'*col.br* (Wol)   21 lig e' d'*sb* (Wol)   22-31 missing in Wol   22 undotted *L* (Pet)   30 *col* (Fl229, Sev)   31 lig (BQ16)   32 *br,* 2*sb* (BQ17)   36/2 no *m.c.* (BQ16, Fl178, Fl229, Sev, Pet)   41 lig (BQ16, BQ17)   46 *br* (BQ17, Wol)   *Contra* 2 lig (BQ16)   5 lig f' g'*br* (Wol)   7/1 no *m.c.* (BQ16, BQ17, Fl178, Fl229, Sev, Pet)   7/2 g'? (Fl176 - ambiguous)   7/3 d'? (Fl178 - ambiguous)   10 *col* (Sev, CG)   11/1 c'*dot.sm* b*f* (BQ16)   12 lig d' *dot.sb* e' *sb* (BQ16)   13/3 lig (Fl229)   16/1 *m.c.* (CG, Wol)   18 2*sb* (Fl176)   20 no lig (Fl178, Sev, CG)   31 no lig (Fl178, CG, Pet)   32/1 *m.c.* (CG)   33/4 *m.c.* (Sev, CG)   36/1 e'*mn* (Sev)   37 lig (Wol)   39/1 *m.c.* (BQ17)   41 no lig (BQ17, Fl178, CG, Wol)   42/2 *m.c.* (CG, Wol)   45/2 *m.c.* (BQ17, CG)   46 no lig (Wol, Pet); c'*dot.sb* b c'*sm* (Sev); c'*mn* d'*sb* c'*mn* (Fl178, CG)

Text   Complete in Superius, incipit only in Contra (Fl178); partial texting in Superius, incipits in Tenor and Contra (Sev); incipits in all voices (BQ16, BQ17, Fl229, Wol); incipits in Superius and Contra (Pet); incipit in Superius only (Fl178, CG).

iii. Adieu naturlic leven mijn

Source

Florence, Biblioteca del Conservatorio Luigi Cherubini, MS Basevi 2439, ff. 3v-4. Facsimile in *Basevi Codex, Florence, Biblioteca del Conservatorio, MS 2439,* ed. Honey MECONI (Peer, 1990).

Modern edition

René B. LENAERTS, *Het Nederlands polifonies lied in de zestiende eeuw* (Mechelen, 1933), Supp., p. 21.

Ascription

"Colinet de lannoy".

Text

Incipit only in D, C, T, *"Adieu naturlic leven myn"*.

The music is free of error. A version of the text in several stanzas is preserved in *Een devoot ende profiteleyk boecxken* (Antwerp, 1544), but this appears to be a sacred paraphrase of an older, secular text preserved in a Dutch polyphonic setting dating from before 1500 (see below under *Related works*), of which the first stanza may be older still. Accordingly, only this version of the first stanza is underlaid here. All ficta is editorial.

Adieu naturlic leven mijn;
Adieu solaes ende al mijn vroecht;
Adieu het moet gesceiden sijn.
Adieu doch werelt ende u ondoecht;
Adieu die mi dic hebt verhoeght.
Adieu ende ic wort u ontoghen
Ende diene mag die suver ioecht.
Bi har sal ic nit sijn bedroghen.

Farewell, my earthly pleasures,
Farewell, amusement and all my delight,
Farewell, I have to leave.
Yes, farewell world and your vices.
Farewell, those who so often cheered me up.
Farewell, I will be taken away from you
And will be allowed to serve pure chastity.
By her I will not be deceived.

(*Trans.* Jaap van Benthem)

iv. Related works

Cela sans plus spawned a variety of reworkings by other composers who appear to have taken Colinet's setting as their model. These include Mass settings by Martini and Obrecht. H. HEWITT, *Canti B... op. cit.,* pp. 42-3, includes a list and a discussion of chanson settings by Lebrun and Cardinal Giovanni de' Medici [= Pope Leo X]. To this list may be added

   i) a setting by JAPPART with the title *Cela sans plus ne souffi pas* (Fl. 229, no. 108, ff. 111v-112; modern edition in H. M. BROWN, *A Florentine Chansonnier... op.cit.,* Music volume, pp. 219-20), whose text is presumably a tongue-in-cheek response to Colinet's, and

   ii) St. Gallen, Stiftsbibliothek, Cod. 530, f. 65r. On this anonymous setting and its relationship to another anonymous version in Regensburg C 120, pp. 316-7, see T. WARBURTON, 'Johannes Sicher...' *op. cit.,* which also includes a transcription of the Regensburg version.

Three settings of *Adieu naturlic leven mijn* appear to be independent of Colinet's. They are found in Segovia, Archivio Capitular de la Catedral, Ms without number, f. 164v (with ascription to Elinc); Brussels, Bibliothèque Royale Albert Ier, Ms II.270, ff. 128v-129 (modern edition: Jan Willem BONDA, *De meerstimmige Nederlandse liederen van de vijftiende en zestiende eeuw,* Hilversum, 1996, pp. 620-21); and St. Gall, Stiftsbibliothek, Cod. 461, pp. 74-5 (modern edition: Franz J. GIESBERT, *Ein altes Spielbuch: Liber Fridolini Sicheri,* Mainz, 1936, pp. 86-7).

BIBLIOGRAPHY

Basevi Codex, Florence, Biblioteca del Conservatorio, MS 2439, Introduction by Honey MECONI, Peer: Alamire, 1990.

BONDA, Jan Willem, *De meerstimmige Nederlandse liederen van de vijftiende en zestiende eeuw*, Hilversum: Verloren, 1996.

D'ACCONE, Frank A., 'The Singers of San Giovanni in Florence during the 15th Century', *JAMS*, xiv (1962), pp. 307-358.

—   'Heinrich Isaac in Florence: New and Unpublished Documents', *MQ*, xlix (1963), pp. 464-83.

—   'The Musical Chapel at the Florentine Cathedral and Baptistery during the First Half of the 16th Century', *JAMS*, xxiv (1971), pp. 1-50.

Déploration de Guillaume Crétin sur le trépas de Jean Ockeghem, ed. Ernest THOINAN, Paris: A. Claudin, 1864 (*R* London: H. Baron, 1965).

A Florentine Chansonnier from the Time of Lorenzo the Magnificent. Florence, Biblioteca Nazionale Centrale, MS Banco Rari 229, ed Howard Mayer BROWN, Chicago and London: University of Chicago Press, 1983, Music Volume, pp. 198-200 (Coll. "MRM", vii).

GIESBERT, Franz J., *Ein altes Spielbuch: Liber Fridolini Sicheri*, Mainz: Schott, 1936.

GOMBOSI, Otto, *Jacob Obrecht: Eine stilkritische Studie*, Leipzig: Breitkopf und Härtel, 1925.

HIGGINS, Paula M., 'Tracing the Careers of Late Medieval Composers: the Case of Philippe Basiron of Bourges', *AM*, lxii (1990), pp. 1-28.

KIRKMAN, Andrew, *The Three-Voice Mass in the Later Fifteenth and Early Sixteenth Centuries: Style, Distribution and Case-Studies*, New York and London: Garland, 1995.

LENAERTS, René B., *Het Nederlands polifonies lied in de zestiende eeuw*, Mechelen-Amsterdam: Het Kompas, 1933, Supp., p. 21.

LOCKWOOD, Lewis, *Music in Renaissance Ferrara 1400-1505*, Oxford: Clarendon Press, 1984.

LOWINKSY, Edward E., 'Ascanio Sforza's Life: A Key to Josquin's Biography and an Aid to the Chronology of his Works', *Josquin Desprez. Proceedings of the International Josquin Festival-Conference, New York City, 21-25 June 1971*, ed. Edward E. LOWINSKY, London: Oxford University Press, 1976.

MITCHELL, Robert J., 'The Palaeography and Repertory of Trent Codices 89 and 91, together with Analyses and Editions of Six Mass Cycles by Franco-Flemish Composers from Trent Codex 89', Ph.D. dissertation, University of Exeter, 1989.

New Obrecht Edition, ed. Chris MAAS *et al.*, Utrecht: Koninklijke Vereniging voor Nederlandse Muziekgeschiedenis, 1983–.

Ottaviano Petrucci, Canti B numero cinquanta, ed. Helen HEWITT, with Introduction by Edward E. LOWINSKY, texts edited by Morton W. BRIGGS and translated by Norman B. SPECTOR, Chicago and London: University of Chicago Press, 1967 (Coll. "MRM", ii).

PERKINS, Leeman L., 'Musical Patronage at the Royal Court of France under Charles VII and Louis XI (1422-1483)' *JAMS*, xxxvii (1984), pp. 507-66.

REYNOLDS, Christopher A., *Papal Patronage and the Music of Saint Peter's*, Berkeley, Los Angeles and London: University of California Press, 1995.

— 'The Origins of San Pietro B 80 and the Development of a Roman Sacred Liturgy, *EMH*, i (1981), pp. 257-304.

Vatican City, Biblioteca Apostolica Vaticana, San Pietro B 80, Introduced by Christopher A. REYNOLDS, New York and London: Garland, 1986 (Coll. "RMF", xxiii).

WARBURTON, Thomas, 'Sicher's "Johannes Zela Zons Plus": A Problem of Identity', *AM*, lv (1983), pp. 74-89.

WEGMAN, Rob C., 'An Anonymous Twin to Johannes Ockeghem's *Missa Quinti Toni* in San Pietro B 80', *TVNM*, xxxvii (1987), pp. 23-48.

Werken van Jacob Obrecht, Wereldlijke Werke, ed. Johannes WOLF, Amsterdam and Leipzig: Vereniging voor Nederlandse Muziekgeschiedenis, 1908-21 (*R* Farnborough: Gregg Press, 1968).

WOLF, Johannes, *Handbuch der Notationskunde*, 2 vols., Leipzig: Breitkopf & Härtel, 1913, (*R* Hildesheim: Georg Olms 1963), I: p. 395.

ACKNOWLEDGMENTS

THANKS ARE DUE to Gareth Curtis for his advice with regard to the text-underlay in the Credo of the Mass; to Andrew Kirkman, for discussing with me its stylistic aspects; to Rob C. Wegman, for making available unpublished materials and for his advice on the matter of ficta and its presentation in *Cela sans plus*; to Jaap van Benthem, for elucidating the question of the text of *Adieu naturlic leven mijn*, and for providing a translation; to Philippe Vendrix and Frank Dobbins for commenting on the final draft of the text; and to David Fallows for the loan of materials, and for his advice on all aspects of this edition. Naturally, the final responsibility rests with me.

THE MASS

Credo in unum Deum

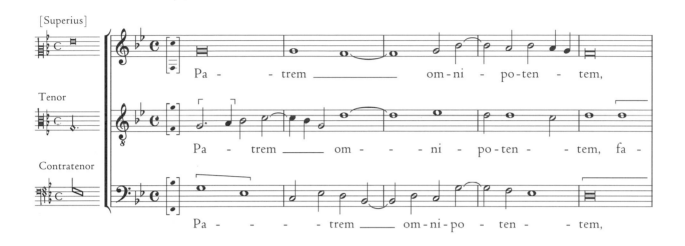

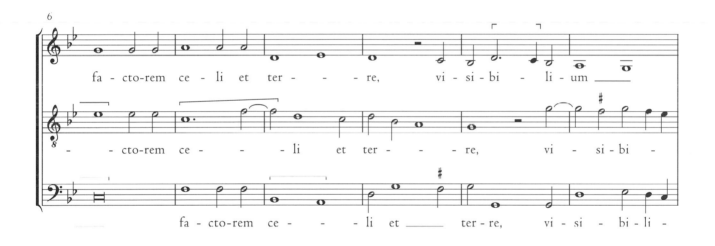

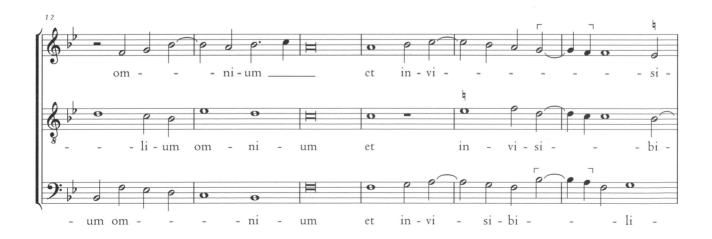

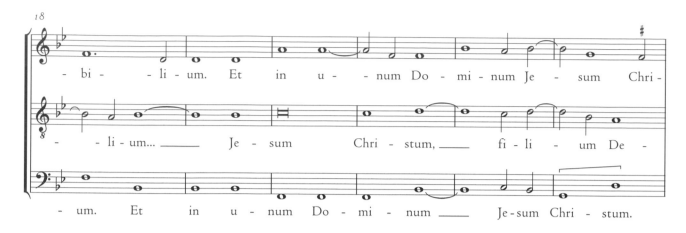

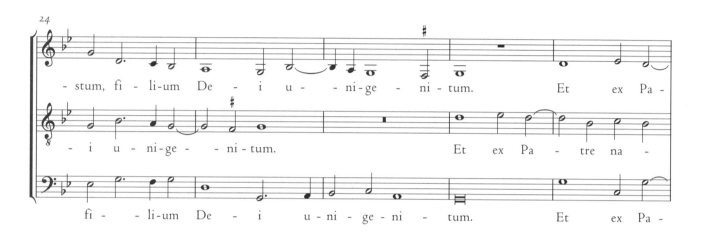

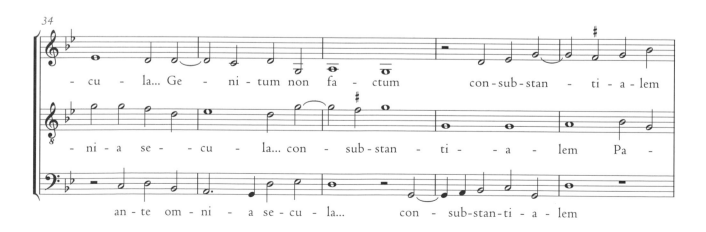

Pa - tri: per - - - quem ___ om - ni - a ___ fa - cta sunt.

- tri: per - quem om - ni - a ___ fa - - cta sunt.

Pa - - tri: ___ per - quem om - ni - a fa - - cta sunt.

Qui pro-pter ___ nos ho - - - - - mi - nes et pro-pter no-stram sa - lu -

Qui pro-pter nos ho - - mi - nes ___ et pro-pter

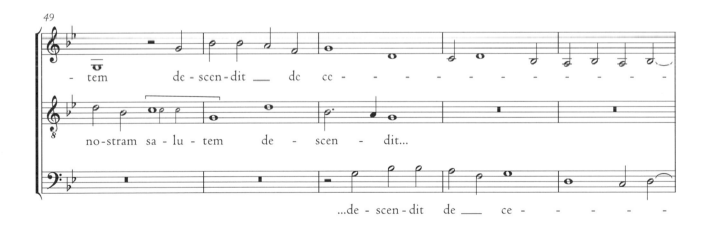

- - - - - tem de - scen-dit ___ de ce - - - - - - -

no-stram sa - lu - tem de - scen - dit...

...de - scen-dit de ___ ce - - - - -

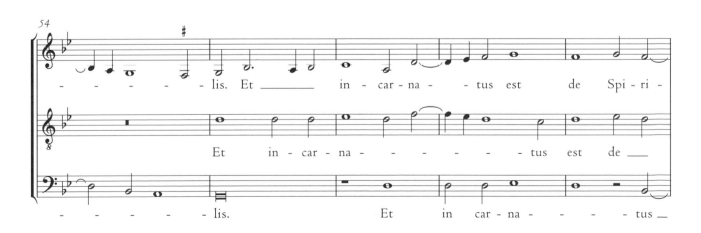

- - - - - lis. Et ___ in - car - na - - tus est de Spi - ri -

Et in - car - na - - - - tus est de ___

- - - - lis. Et in - car - na - - tus ___

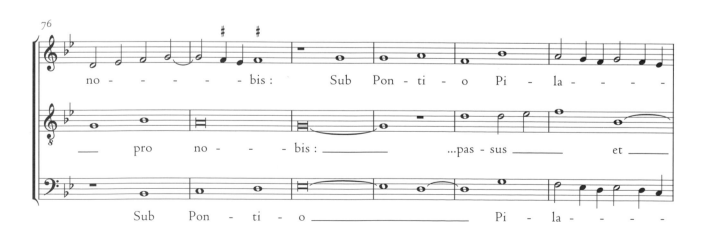

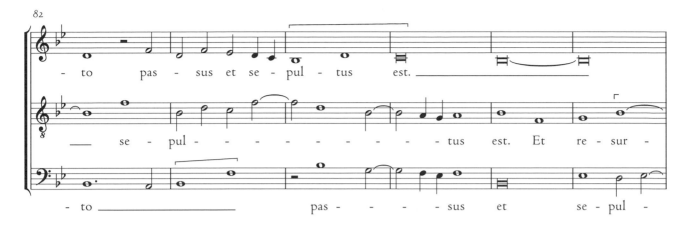

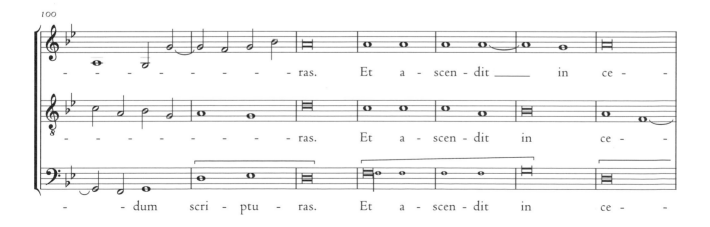

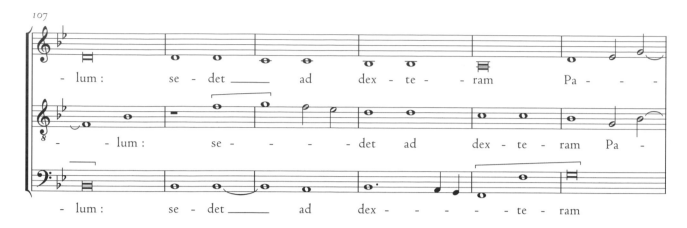

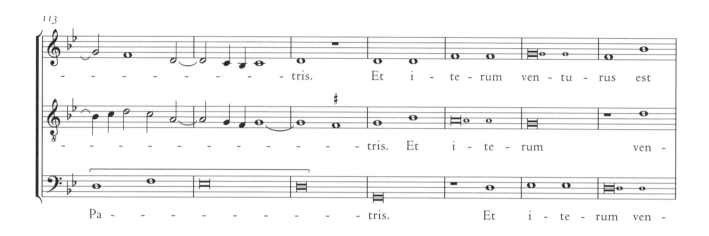

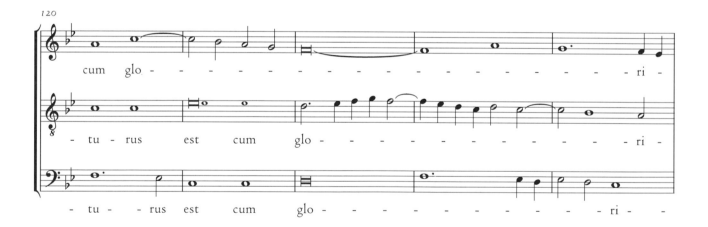

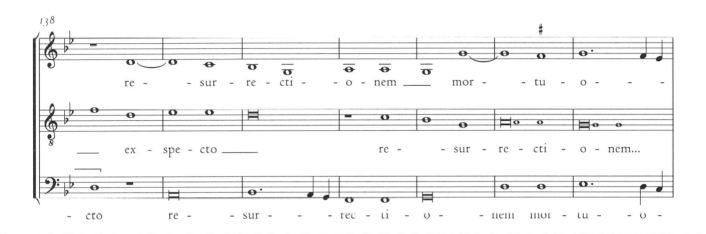

Sanctus

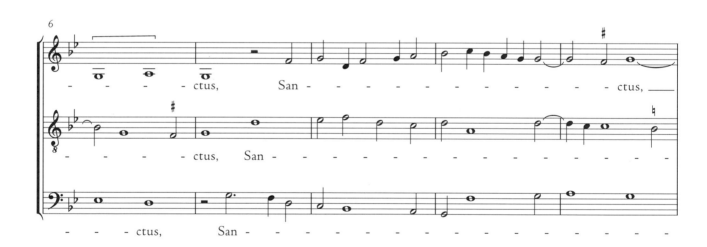

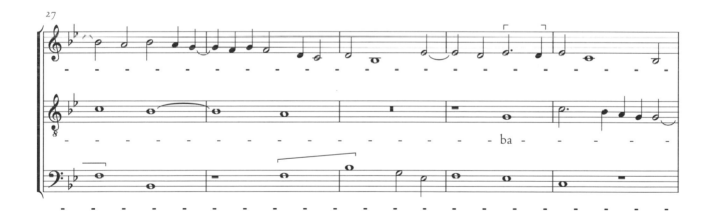

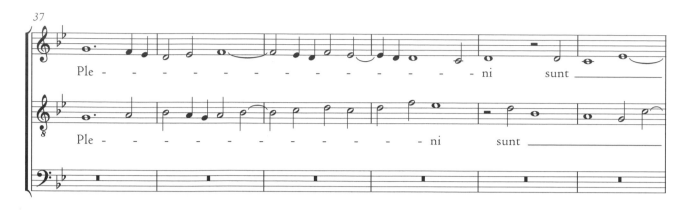

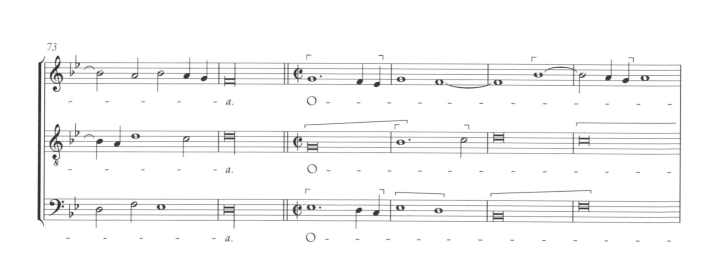

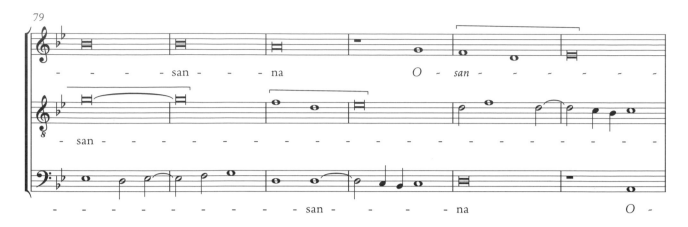

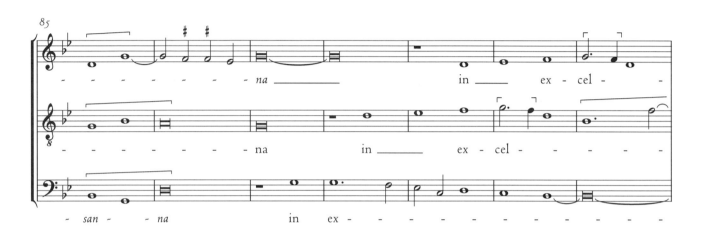

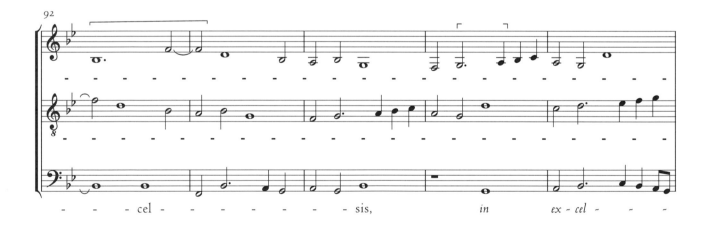

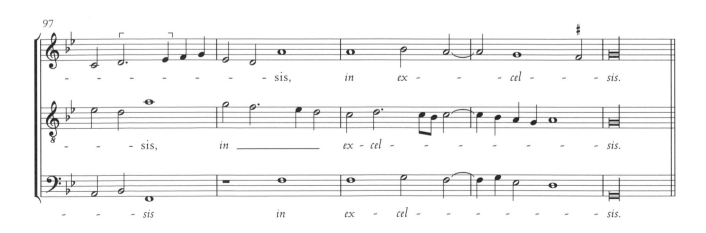

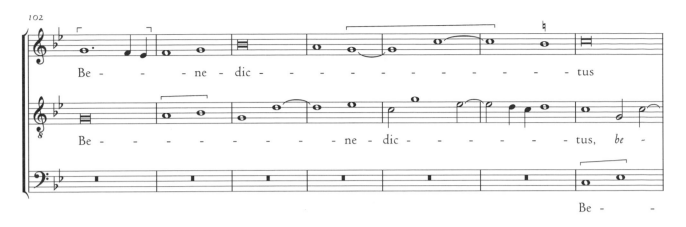

Be - - ne - dic - - - - - - - - - - tus

Be - - - - - - ne - dic - - - - - tus, be -

Be -

qui ve - -

- - ne - dic - - - - - tus

- - - - - - - - - - ne - dic - - - - - -

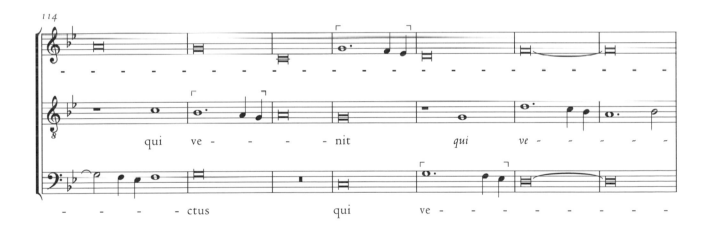

- - - - - - - - - - - - - - -

qui ve - - - nit qui ve - - - - - -

- - - - ctus qui ve - - - - - - - -

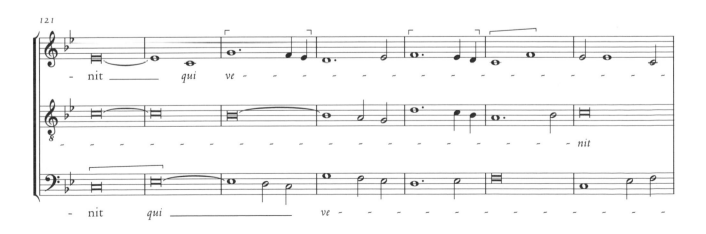

- nit _____ qui ve - - - - - - - - - - - - - - - -

- - - - - - - - - - - nit

- nit qui _____ ve - - - - - - - - -

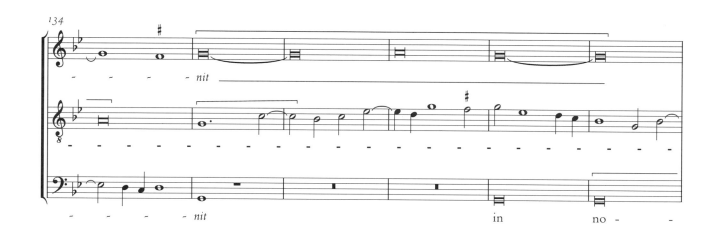

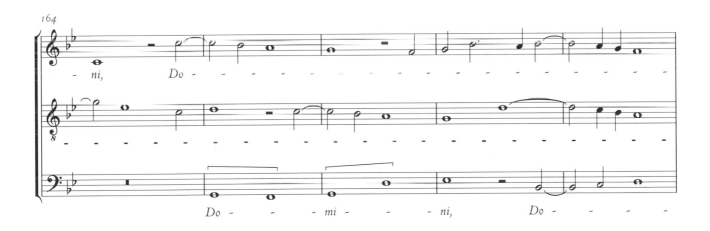

[Osanna ut supra]

Agnus Dei

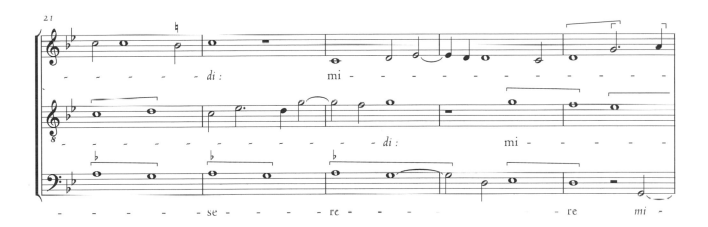

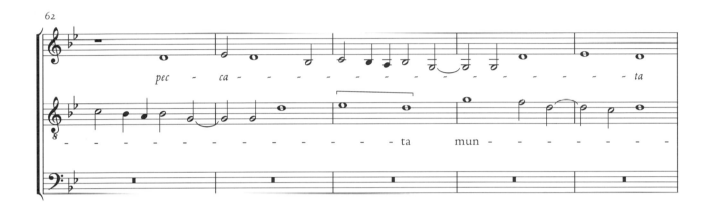

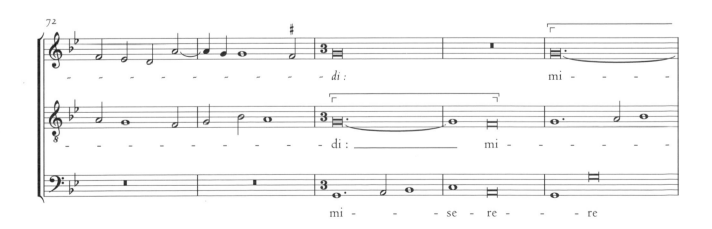

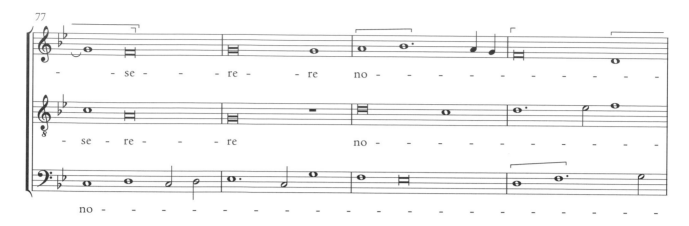

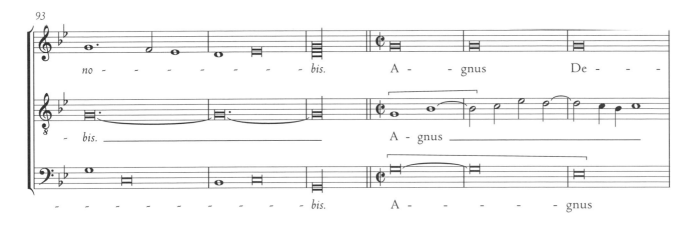

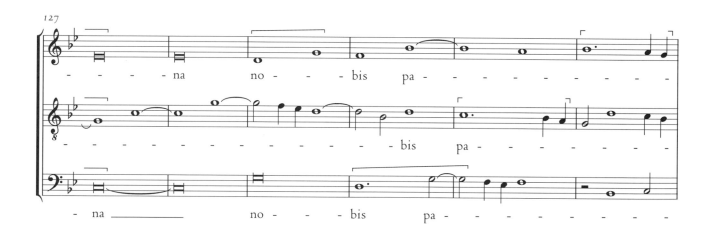

SONGS

Cela sans plus

(1) Wol   (2) Fl176   (3) Fl176, Fl229

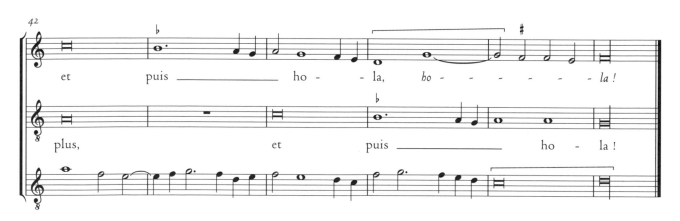

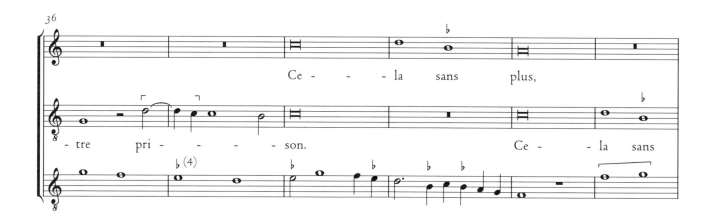

(4) BQ16, Fl176, Fl229, CG, Pet

Adieu naturlic leven mijn

A - dieu het _____ mœt _____ ge - scei -

- - den sijn. A - dieu doch we - - - - - - -

- relt ende _____ u _____ on - doecht.

A - dieu die mi — dic hebt _____ ver -

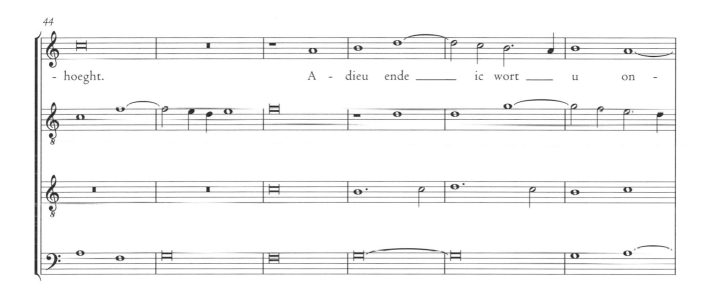

- hoeght. A - dieu ende _____ ic wort ____ u on -

- -to - ghen. Ende die - ne mag _____

die su - - ver ioecht. Bi har sal ic nit

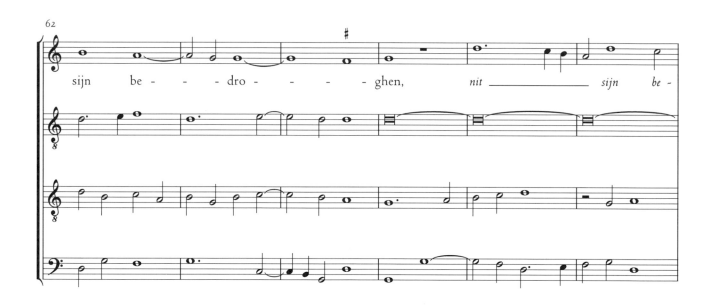

sijn be - - dro - - - ghen, nit _____ sijn be -

- dro - - - - - - - - - ghen. _____

ACHEVÉ D'IMPRIMER
EN FÉVRIER 1999
SUR LES PRESSES
DE
L'IMPRIMERIE F. PAILLART
À ABBEVILLE

DÉPÔT LÉGAL : 1er TRIMESTRE 1999
N° D'IMP. 10591